VIDEO GAME
MUSIC

CLASSIC *f*M
HANDY
GUIDES

VIDEO GAME
MUSIC

DANIEL ROSS

First published 2015 by
Elliott and Thompson Limited
27 John Street
London WC1N 2BX
www.eandtbooks.com

ISBN: 978-1-90965-366-5

Text © Classic FM 2015

9 8 7 6 5 4 3 2 1

A catalogue record for this book is available from the
British Library.

Typesetting: Marie Doherty
Printed in the UK by TJ International Ltd

Contents

Introduction   vii
Preface   ix

1 From the Arcade to the Home   1
2 The Arrival of Orchestral Scores   17
3 The Record Industry   29
4 Video Game Music in the Concert Hall   39
5 Mobile Gaming, Online and the Future   53
6 20 Essential Video Game Music Scores   73

About Classic FM   87
About the Author   91
Index   93

Introduction

At Classic FM, we spend a lot of our time dreaming up wonderful ways of making sure that as many people as possible across the UK have the opportunity to listen to classical music. As the nation's biggest classical music radio station, we feel that we have a responsibility to share the world's greatest music as widely as we can.

Over the years, we have written a variety of classical music books in all sorts of shapes and sizes. But we have never put together a series of books quite like this.

This set of books covers a whole range of aspects of classical music. They are all written in Classic FM's friendly, accessible style and you can rest assured that they are packed full of facts about classical music. Read separately, each book gives you a handy snapshot of a particular subject area. Added together, the series combines to offer a more detailed insight into the full story of classical music. Along the way, we shall be paying particular attention to some of the key composers whose music we play most often on the radio station, as well as examining many of classical music's subgenres.

These books are relatively small in size, so they are not going to be encyclopedic in their level of detail; there are other books out there that do that much better than we could ever hope to. Instead, they are intended to be enjoyable introductory guides that will be particularly useful to listeners who are beginning their voyage of discovery through the rich and exciting world of classical music. Drawing on the research we have undertaken for many of our previous Classic FM books, they concentrate on information rather than theory because we want to make this series of books attractive and inviting to readers who are not necessarily familiar with the more complex aspects of musicology.

For more information on this series, take a look at our website: www.ClassicFM.com/handyguides.

Preface

You'd be forgiven for thinking video game music is nothing more than a series of beeps, designed to accompany pixelated images of Italian plumbers or electric-haired hedgehogs jumping around and collecting coins and rings for points. Alas, for Super Mario and Sonic the Hedgehog respectively, this was certainly the case in the early days. But since the late 1990s, a sea change has occurred and the retro-sounding, eight-bit loops of music have become objects of nostalgia. Nowadays, the multi-billion-pound video game industry is responsible for commissioning enough orchestral scores to rival Hollywood, and its composers are increasingly treated with the same reverence. Some of today's top movie composers actually started their professional careers as composers for video games and countless new composers manage to operate in both mediums with terrific success.

Perhaps most notably, a massive, communal and international fan culture has emerged, which ensures that enthusiasm for video game music remains at a constant fever pitch. Huge concert tours that focus on specific games series sell out huge auditoriums all over the world in mere hours (both the *Final Fantasy* and *The Legend of Zelda* franchises are a popular concert draw) and attendees display due reverence to composers and games alike by turning up in fancy dress and singing along with their favourite excerpts. Thanks to this atmosphere, which is truly unlike any other in the classical music world, video game music concerts look to be a safe bet in this time of wobbling ticket sales and budgetary constrictions.

If you require any greater verification of video game music's here-to-stay status, you need only look at the Classic FM Hall of Fame, the world's biggest annual classical music survey. In 2012, for the first time ever, two video game scores turned up in the all-important Top 300 – Nobuo Uematsu's *Final Fantasy* and Jeremy Soule's *The Elder Scrolls*. Then, in 2013, they went Top 5 – *Final Fantasy* climbed into the No. 3 position and *The Elder Scrolls* landed at No. 5, beating the mighty Beethoven down into No. 6 (and the resulting heated online debates about whether it counts as 'proper' classical music continue to this day). It's important not to under-estimate this development, as it signals a massive shift. Video game music is no longer the preserve of the nerds – it's crossed over into the mainstream and is now a lucrative, inventive and continually growing area of music.

It hasn't always been like this, though. There really was a time when video game scores were confined to just a few different sounds per game. The limited memory space available restricted what any 'normal' composer would be able to achieve in terms of recording, instruments and just about everything else that could make a piece of music more expressive.

In this book, we're going to focus on the evolu-tion of video game music as an orchestral format and how it became a firm fixture of the genre. As a result we'll be skipping over most of the more elec-tronic and 'chiptune' scores, but it's worth briefly mentioning some of the early electronic innovators and their restrictions, as it was those restrictions that actually helped some of the more successful composers to become more inventive. Tellingly, it's those composers who have managed to survive the transition to full orchestral compositions.

But to start, we have to travel, perhaps inevitably, to Japan in the late 1970s and the world of arcade games ...

one

From the Arcade to the Home

Imagine the noise of a video games arcade and you'll probably hear the electronic whoops, beeps and whistles of sound effects, and perhaps the occasional tune that signified the beginning of a new level. Genre classics such as *Pac-Man* (1980) had a recognisable theme composed by the game's sound director Toshio Kai, but examples like this were confined by the computer chips that held them – simply, the arcade machines couldn't cope with anything more complicated than a couple of sounds at a time. If a game developer wanted to include music in his magnum opus, it had to be programmed in, and not necessarily by anyone with any musical training. Unsurprisingly, the use of music was almost a millstone around the neck of your average game developer in the 1970s and 80s.

An early pioneer, though, was the iconic *Space Invaders*, made by Japanese gaming giant Taito in 1978. Game developer (note: not composer) **Tomohiro Nishikado** (born in 1944) was among the first to create a theme that could be heard while the game itself was being played. Well, perhaps 'theme' is a strong word. Essentially, the player would hear the same four notes repeated over and over, gradually becoming faster as the enemy swooped closer and closer to the player. What's crucial here, though, is that the music, such as it was, was audible *during* gameplay, not just between levels. Still, having only one melodic line to play with at a time was a huge restriction on what composers could do and it wasn't until later in the 1980s that the technology to use more than one note at a time developed.

In 1981, *Frogger* (made by Konami) contained several different themes for various points during the game and even changed to reflect the player's outcome (those of a certain age and with a misspent youth will remember the thrill of getting your frogs across the road and the subsequent change in musical theme). The composer of said themes is sadly anonymous, suggesting that again perhaps a slightly more musically minded developer is responsible. Other games, such as 1982's *Dig Dug* (a Namco classic), also contained multiple themes, some of them distinctly Baroque in sound, but there were still severe compositional restrictions thanks to the limitations of the sound technology available. Strangely enough, this stunted style of music has continued to have immense appeal to enthusiasts, and musicians still use 'chiptune', as it was eventually termed, in plenty of alternative pop and dance music today to inject a certain nostalgia into their recordings.

Things were, however, still a great distance from the orchestral scores that we've come to appreciate today. Major technical innovation would be required to allow the genre to grow, which started with games moving out of the arcade and into the home.

The Arrival of Consoles

When gaming moved out of the arcade and into the home thanks to consoles such as the Commodore 64 (released in 1982) and Nintendo's Famicom (released in 1983 and later to become better known as the Nintendo Entertainment System, or NES), so the musical capabilities of the machinery started to become a little more serious. Two names that have gone on to achieve legendary status in the video game music industry are **Koji Kondo** (born in 1961) and **Nobuo Uematsu** (born in 1959), thanks to their music composed for the *Super Mario Bros.* and *Final Fantasy* games franchises respectively.

Another leading light in the early days of video game music was **Koichi Sugiyama** (born in 1931), who composed the main themes for the popular role-playing game (known as RPGs in the business) *Dragon Quest I* in 1986. Sugiyama wore his classical influences on his sleeve and, remarkably, his soundtrack became the first to be re-recorded by a full symphony orchestra, with the London Philharmonic Orchestra playing on the 1986 CD release of the game's main themes. Of course, the sound in the original SNES (Super Nintendo Entertainment System) version was still limited by technology, but a seed had been planted. Indeed, Sugiyama's role in the birth of live video game music concerts was to eclipse his popularity as a composer in the story of the genre – but we'll come back to that later.

Koji Kondo's Link to Greatness

Kondo's *Super Mario Bros.* theme from 1985 took advantage of the increased memory power of Nintendo's NES/Famicom and its not insubstantial five available channels of sound, and kicked off a game music revolution. That theme, with its bouncy, approachable feel, has become completely synonymous with the moustachioed Italian plumber it represents, in exactly the same way that John Williams' theme for the movie version of *Superman* did with the eponymous tights-wearing superhero in the 1970s.

Kondo was also notable in that he was the first composer ever hired by the gaming giants at Nintendo, where he continues to work to this day – an investment that has seen him create many further *Super Mario* game scores into the new millennium. His main theme for *Super Mario Bros.* has been orchestrated and performed by countless orchestras in recent years, ensuring that his compositions have made the full transition from chiptune to symphonic piece.

Another success for Kondo came with *The Legend of Zelda*. These games have a very special place in the industry. Another Nintendo title

(Nintendo are the granddaddies of the gaming industry, having created such series as *Super Mario*, *Donkey Kong* and *Pokémon*), the *Zelda* franchise kicked off back in 1986 with its first game for the NES, subtitled *The Hyrule Fantasy*. Much of the gameplay focuses on the main character, a boy named Link, who spends the majority of his time roaming around a fantastical woodland landscape trying to locate and save the titular Princess Zelda. It's an immersive, story-led game in the RPG genre and the Nintendo team worked on it at the same time as it was putting the finishing touches to the first *Super Mario Bros.* game. As a result, it's almost the complete opposite of *Mario* – focusing on strong story elements and a slower rate of gameplay that championed puzzle-solving and emotional investment in the characters.

But despite this first game's legendary place in the industry thanks to all its technical and storytelling innovations, it's arguably Kondo's soundtrack that has stood the test of time most successfully. In its initial incarnation for the NES, the famous main theme is a folky, two-line melody in the familiar electronic sound of the console's limited musical voice. But it is beautifully, logically composed and, with the benefit of hindsight, it really does sound as if it could be scored for a full orchestra. Of course, that is eventually what happened as the video game music world became stronger and more inclined to revive older scores, but Kondo's original theme and several that occur throughout the early games in the series have very clear orchestral potential.

That main theme, though, almost didn't make it into the game. Kondo's original plan was to simply reduce and rescore French composer Maurice Ravel's epic orchestral masterpiece *Boléro* for the game's title screen, but at the crucial moment he discovered that the piece was still in copyright and, unless a hefty licensing fee could be found, he'd have to can the idea. So, with no little desperation, he supposedly composed the game's main theme in just one day. Whether that's true or not, it's yet more evidence that video game music composers were striving for that orchestral dimension, that sense of bombast and event that only orchestral scores can provide.

Kondo's *Zelda* music has since become the subject of many dedicated live performances and the later instalments in the series (perhaps most notably in 1998's *The Legend of Zelda: Ocarina of Time*) rely heavily on music to trigger actual gameplay elements – learning and playing tunes in the game can unlock certain plot developments and secrets. But at the time of the early entries in the Zelda series – innovative though they were in terms of story, gameplay and music – greater interactivity and sophistication was still to come.

Nobuo Uematsu – The Gamer's Richard Wagner?

If composers such as Kondo and Sugiyama were among the first to take steps towards video game music being accepted as seriously as film soundtracks or even classical music itself, then Uematsu was the man who grabbed the baton and sprinted for the finish line. Uematsu (a self-taught pianist, Elton John fan and music-shop employee) composed his first *Final Fantasy* score in 1987 for game developers Square, and changed video game music for ever. The music still sounded lo-fi, the bleeps were still defiantly bleepy, but the music itself strived for the complexity and sensitivity of a full orchestral work.

Much like Richard Wagner did in his epic

operas of the nineteenth century, Uematsu assigned different themes to different characters in the games, which themselves were almost Tolkienesque in their fantastical scope and range of characters. This kind of RPG married perfectly with Uematsu's symphonic leanings and a strange middle ground was struck between classical pastiche, classic Hollywood film scoring and those omnipresent chiptune sounds. Uematsu's career has, in many ways, been defined by his ongoing work on the *Final Fantasy* series (currently on its fourteenth instalment with several spin-offs besides), which has seen him finally realise his intentions of having his music played by a full symphony orchestra in the games themselves.

Games on CD

As small tweaks to home gaming continued to occur in the 1980s and into the early 1990s, so the accompanying music and its composers carried on as they had been doing. The arrival of 16-bit consoles including the Sega Mega Drive and the SNES meant that music could become more elaborate and up to ten sounds could be heard at once – in stereo, no less. Game developers began to experiment with pre-recorded music as well as music composed especially for their games, and a prevailing taste for techno- and dance-influenced soundtracks began to take hold. Theme songs and vocals began to crop up as much as the more instrumental Uematsu and Sugiyama orchestral models. Increasingly, movie tie-in games would feature rearranged versions of their popular main themes, such as Williams' *Jurassic Park* and *Star Wars*.

A huge change, however, was on the horizon. The so-called 'fifth generation' of home video game consoles began using CDs as a common vehicle for games, rather than cartridges – which meant CD-quality sound. Arriving on the market in 1994, Sony's groundbreaking PlayStation could support a whopping twenty-four channels of sound. Recorded songs were now staples of gameplay, those film tie-in games were suddenly resplendent with the original symphonic recordings of their themes, and all was geared towards a bright, orchestral future. But one key ingredient was missing – the perfect game to hang a full-scale, movie-style soundtrack on. Well, the missing ingredient turned up in 1997 – *Final Fantasy VII*.

Nobuo Uematsu's Magnum Opus:
Final Fantasy VII

Unsurprisingly, after quickly establishing himself as a major player in the world of video game music, Uematsu was at the forefront of the so-called fifth generation of home gaming consoles (Sony's PlayStation, Nintendo's N64 and Sega's Saturn). By 1997, the *Final Fantasy* series was up to its sixth entry. *Final Fantasy VII*, released originally for the Sony PlayStation, has given video game music fans some of the most recognisable moments in the genre, buoyed an entire industry of live concerts and firmly plonked itself near the business end of the Classic FM Hall of Fame. Interestingly, given the technology now available to Uematsu, he didn't opt for a costly, complex symphony orchestra when it came to composing *Final Fantasy VII*. Instead, he decided that pre-programmed MIDI (Musical Instrument Digital Interface – basically more bleepy sounds) instruments would be enough, but he held on to that all-important orchestral scope.

More than any video game soundtrack before it, *Final Fantasy VII* embraced the notion that video game music should serve the same function as film music. And with this particular role-playing game, it made perfect sense. The plot, which unfolds over something like forty hours of gameplay, concerns the quest of a band of characters in a far-off planet to bring an evil electricity corporation to justice and the ultimate conflict between them and Sephiroth, an ex-soldier hell-bent on world domination (it makes perfect sense when you play it). Putting it mildly, there was plenty of material for an eager composer to get his thematic teeth into.

Uematsu again assigned different musical melodies and segments to the main characters, locations and themes, in the same way that Wagner and Williams had done before him. The most notable of these, 'Aerith's Theme', will be known to Classic FM listeners as the piece that stormed the Top 5 of the Hall of Fame in 2013, but there are several different themes here that are comparable to the most memorable of movie themes. The climactic 'One-Winged Angel', for example, has a bizarre choral intensity to it, with Uematsu claiming to have been influenced equally by Igor Stravinsky and Jimi Hendrix.

Technically, another distinguishing feature of *Final Fantasy VII* was its extensive use of Full Motion Videos (known in the business as FMVs), which bookended key segments of the game. Essentially they're sections of video comparable to computer-animated movies that, naturally, required music in exactly the same way. Uematsu, rather than just composing repetitive themes for these sections, completely embraced their filmic quality and approached them in the same way a film composer would. Dazzling action sequences and fantastical visuals were now equalled by their scores, which were every bit as impressive. FMVs are now the industry standard when it comes to presentation, but Uematsu was among the very first to capitalise on their musical potential.

This melting pot of influences, the rapidly catching-up audio technology and the arrival of a game with themes epic enough to warrant such a huge soundtrack undertaking created the perfect storm. *Final Fantasy VII* remains one of the most critically acclaimed video games of all time and has sold well over 10 million copies worldwide. As a result, Uematsu's themes were now sewn into the canvas of video game music as a genre and, crucially, there was a huge audience for them. There had been successes before, but never one as global as this.

Games Like Movies

Operating alongside the *Final Fantasy* series was another epic of the RPG genre, the *Ys* series. Pronounced 'ee-su' and released originally on the NEC PC-8801 home computer in Japan, it has a similar history to *Final Fantasy*, but as yet still hasn't taken off globally in the same way, despite new instalments now being released in Western markets. What these giants of Japanese gaming culture do share, though, is a distinctly cinematic aesthetic and story arc, and a fantastical setting. Musically, the energetic themes of composer **Yuzo Koshiro** (born in 1967) for early games in the series (it kicked off in 1987 with *Ys I: Ancient Ys Vanished*) were dominated by purposefully 'poppy' electronic sounds, with occasional toe-in-the-water visits to orchestral instruments.

Koshiro would later wow the soundtrack world again with his work on the influential Sega Dreamcast title *Shenmue* in 1999, but his role was actually bigger than these titles alone. What his role shows is that this cinematic style of gaming, where players are encouraged to be involved in complex, emotional storylines for long periods of time, was becoming commonplace, even standard. This is

fundamental for the soundtracks and their composers – video game music was going to have to step
up and soundtrack a range of emotional situations,
not merely provide background bleeps for shoot-
ing things. If video games were going to be taken
seriously as an artform, then the music needed to
share that goal of complete, emotional immersion.
Composers such as Koshiro and Uematsu were key
to this transition.

More to the point, the Western world was now
seeing just what the Japanese game developers and
composers had been doing, and it was time for
them to compete. The US and Europe, with their
by now formidable history of film music and classical music, was surely poised to make some serious
contributions to the genre too.

two

The Arrival
of Orchestral Scores

It's perhaps unfair to say that the Western world of video game music had some catching up to do, but it can't be denied that the focus, until the late 1990s, had very much been on Japan and its burgeoning orchestral prowess. As we established, Japan had created something resembling a first wave of video game music, thanks to Uematsu, Kondo, Sugiyama and Koshiro.

What the US and Europe had going in their favour, however, was a huge boom in video game sales as the 1990s proceeded, and the lucrative prospect of movie tie-ins. Williams' music for monster-selling movies and franchises such as *Star Wars, ET: The Extra-Terrestrial* and others had been scaled down to soundtrack the more lo-fi sounds of the 1980s and 90s video game market, but with CD technology and high-quality audio becoming a standard on home consoles, the idea of putting an orchestral soundtrack to a home video game was now turning into a reality.

The John Williams Effect

It's worth noting the huge effect that film soundtrack composer and all-round Hollywood legend **John Williams** (born in 1932) has had on video game music, perhaps without him really realising it. As the movie industry gradually began to tap into the potential of movie tie-in video games, Williams' music has played a big part in the video games industry. A very healthy proportion of all the films that Williams scores gets turned into video games at one point or another and, logically, his music goes with it. It's been that way since his scores for the early *Star Wars* films and it's happened with titles as diverse as *ET: The Extra-Terrestrial*, *Superman* and the *Indiana Jones* and *Harry Potter* series.

As we'll find out in this chapter, Williams' work has meant that there's an orchestral inspiration for newer composers who seek to emulate and recreate the power of film music's emotional resonance in their game soundtracks – sometimes by directly adding to Williams' work for specific games.

The most incredible thing about Williams' effect on the world of video game music, though, must be that, to this day, he has never composed a single note of music especially for the medium. But his influence on composers such as Michael Giacchino has been crucial in the early stages of their careers.

Michael Giacchino: Early Adopter

He's better known nowadays for his work on movie blockbusters such as the *Star Trek* and *Planet of the Apes* franchise reboots (not to mention numerous awards for his work, including scores for *Lost*, *The Incredibles*, and *Up*), but New Jersey native **Michael Giacchino** (born in 1967) began his career as an intern at Universal Pictures in the early 1990s. However, thanks to his tenacity and some classes at the prestigious Juilliard School of Music in New York, he quickly wound up in the heady world of video games at Disney Interactive in Los Angeles, composing music for the movie tie-in release of *The Lion King* in 1994, as well as some smaller titles.

Having proved himself capable of handling prestigious, money-making titles, Giacchino was handed an incredible opportunity – to compose incidental music for the *The Lost World: Jurassic Park* video game, released on Sony PlayStation and Sega Saturn in 1997. Giacchino was to provide new music for the game version of the blockbuster Steven Spielberg movie of the same name to go alongside the themes that Williams had composed for the film's soundtrack, which also featured in the game.

What set this release apart from Giacchino's other work and, indeed, much of the wider industry at the time, was that it used a full symphony orchestra in the recording process. Incredibly, this was something of a fluke, according to Giacchino himself, and an orchestral recording was secured only when Steven Spielberg heard demo versions of the score, asking when he was likely to hear the music recorded properly.

The rest is, as they say, history. Spielberg was instantly impressed by the work that Giacchino did to complement the existing Williams film score, and engaged him once again in 1999 for the first instalment of a brand new series of World War II-based video games that he'd been developing, called *Medal of Honor*. Giacchino, buoyed by the success of his orchestral soundtrack for *The Lost World: Jurassic Park*, composed a compellingly cinematic series of cues for the game, which saw the main character, Jimmy Patterson, represented by two noble themes of his own. The game, a first-person shoot-'em-up, has spawned nearly a dozen sequels and spin-offs, for most of which Giacchino has returned to provide the music.

The natural capacity for video game music to behave in the same way and perform the same function as the music written for a Hollywood movie was given another boost and the number of games with high-budget, high-quality orchestral soundtracks soared.

Giacchino went on to become one of the most sought-after composers in Hollywood, winning an Academy Award in 2010 for his soundtrack to the Disney–Pixar animation *Up*, and working closely with young buck director J. J. Abrams on his TV shows *Lost* and *Alias*, and then his newer contributions to the *Star Trek* franchise. He is, more than any other video game music composer, proof that the music of the games world was rapidly gaining as much cultural credence and clout as the movie world.

Orchestras Everywhere

With a standard of orchestral music in video games now set, the late 1990s and early 2000s became a rich and fertile ground where a once fledgling band of composers could begin to make a stable, fruitful living.

British-born **Harry Gregson-Williams** (born in 1961) and his soundtracks for the later entries in the *Metal Gear Solid* series of espionage thriller games were to become industry standard in terms of their exposure, budget and acclaim. Gregson-Williams, who cut his teeth as an assistant to the great film soundtrack composer Hans Zimmer, didn't let his acclaim as a film music composer put him off dipping a toe into the world of video game music – and he had tremendous success.

The *Metal Gear Solid* series has enjoyed multiple sequels since the first game was released in 1998 (two earlier Japan-only releases in the *Metal Gear* series predate this first proper Western release). A number of other composers have contributed to these later sequels, such as Los Angeles born **Jamie Christopherson** (born in 1975) and **Norihiko Hibino** (born in 1973), giving the whole series an unwieldy range of sounds – it's bound together by a fusion of orchestral bombast, heavily produced electronic sounds and the occasional slushy ballad. The combination of orchestral music with other different styles within the *Metal Gear Solid* series demonstrated that the function of the orchestra in game music by the end of the twentieth century was really quite similar to its role in film music – to serve the game's ever-changing story and aesthetic as needed.

More left-field, ambient examples of orchestration and soundtracking in video games began to emerge as the capacity for experimentation grew. The *Resident Evil* series of games, which began as George Romero-inspired 'survival horror' zombie outbreak adventures, provided early examples of video game music straying from the orchestral mould. The first instalment was released by game developers Capcom in 1996 on Sony PlayStation and was notable for its use of eerie, disjointed music, conjured by Japanese composers Makoto Tomozawa, Akari Kaida, and Masami Ueda.

The soundtrack to the original *Resident Evil* sounds rather dated nowadays, with its industrial sound effects and occasional bursts of synthesizer and rock beats, but the sequels, *Resident Evil 2* and *Resident Evil 3: Nemesis*, display a much more sophisticated use of sound. Masami Ueda's, Shusaku Uchiyama's and Syun Nishigaki's use of high, screechy strings and occasional flurries of thundering percussion is far more cinematic and actually sounds closer to Bernard Herrmann's legendary scores for Alfred Hitchcock's movie thrillers, such as *Psycho* and *North by Northwest*.

The *Resident Evil* games' music became popular enough to warrant its own orchestral concert in 1999 with the New Japan Philharmonic Orchestra playing this chilling, sophisticated music to a live audience. The subsequent live recording of the concert has gone on to have a life of its own, and was re-released in the US in 2001.

Music for games such as *Halo: Combat Evolved* (popularly known simply as *Halo*) took this broad approach even further, with composers **Martin O'Donnell** (born in 1955) and **Michael Salvatori** (born in 1954) claiming they wanted their soundtrack for the hugely popular shoot-'em-up to sound like 'a little Samuel Barber meets [electro and disco pioneer] Giorgio Moroder'.

Halo is in itself a benchmark game that spawned a seemingly unending series of sequels and add-ons to cope with the huge fan demand (originally released in 2001, it's estimated that the series has sold over 50 million units worldwide). The themes composed for the game have become equally beloved, with the choral-inspired soundtrack album being released to acclaim (and not inconsiderable sales) in 2002.

Jeremy Soule: Striking Out Alone

Thanks to the demand for orchestral sounds in video games, composers such as Iowa-born **Jeremy Soule** (born in 1975) soon became big names in the industry, and Soule in particular has come to represent the journey from left field to mainstream.

Soule's contribution to the world of game soundtracks began as early as 1994 when he was employed as a composer by the US arm of Japanese gaming giant Square (the company that was responsible for the *Final Fantasy* series). Early successes such as 1995's *Secret of Evermore*, an adventure game where the player's role alternates between a boy and a shape-shifting dog (obviously), utilised minimal sounds and simple scores, not entirely reminiscent of the orchestral sound that characterises his more recent works.

The turning point came in 2000 when Soule, riding the success of composing the award-winning score to the popular PC war strategy game *Total Annihilation* (which jostled with Giacchino's *The Lost World* soundtrack as one of the earliest orchestral video game soundtracks in 1997), founded his own production company dedicated to making soundtracks. Soule Media, later to become Artistry Entertainment, was formed with Soule's brother Julian, and has been responsible for producing all of Jeremy's landmark scores.

Scores such as *The Elder Scrolls III: Morrowind* (2002) considerably developed the epic, orchestral dimension of Soule's writing, containing several rich, lush themes that won the game acclaim (though some accused it of being too short and repetitive). The *Elder Scrolls* series, which is a pioneer in what has become known as 'open world' gaming (basically a game where players can roam freely in a large-scale 3D world, nowadays often based on the Internet), was to be a charm for Soule, and he has either composed the full score or provided themes for each instalment since. Indeed, thanks to the success of the track 'Dragonborn' from *The Elder Scrolls V: Skyrim*, Soule's soundtrack has recently become a fixture in the Classic FM Hall of Fame survey, placing fifth in 2013 and, along with Uematsu's *Final Fantasy* at No. 3, pushing Beethoven out of the Top 5.

Just like Giacchino before him, though, Soule has also mined the rich seam of movie tie-ins, composing music for five games in the *Harry Potter* series and also the odd *Star Wars* game as well. (That John Williams effect really does have a wide reach, doesn't it?) Interestingly, recent years have seen Soule strive to create something outside the gaming world. In 2012, he launched an online fundraising campaign to record his first 'proper' traditional orchestral symphony, entitled *The Northerner: Soule Symphony No. 1*. His initial target for the project was to raise $10,000. When the fundraising campaign closed on 14 April 2013, a gob-smacking total of $121,227 had been sourced, all from eager fans and consumers, desperate to hear what Soule would come up with when released from the confines of a game soundtrack. If anyone ever needed proof that video game music composers could be counted alongside the symphonic greats of history when it comes to appreciative audiences, then Soule would be a good person for them to chat with.

three

The Record Industry

How do you actually go about listening to a video game soundtrack? Just as it's difficult to really appreciate the full effect of a movie soundtrack unless you buy it separately from the film, a video game soundtrack can't be experienced to the absolute max without turning off the console and putting on your headphones. And, just like the movie soundtrack world, the record industry has made that experience possible. Indeed, sales of video game soundtracks are nowadays substantial enough to propel individual releases and compilations into the upper echelons of the classical charts.

The start of a trend

Beginning, again perhaps unsurprisingly, in Japan, the appeal and subsequent market for video game soundtracks on CD was an early indicator of the genre's popularity. As mentioned back in the first chapter of this book, the soundtrack for *Dragon Quest*, composed by Sugiyama in 1986, was the first ever to be recorded by a full symphony orchestra for release on CD. The recording itself did well enough in the Japanese markets to warrant further recordings of Sugiyama's work, and in the following years live recordings of his work by the Tokyo Philharmonic Orchestra and the NHK Symphony Orchestra emerged.

Following Sugiyama's initiative, a gaggle of eager video game music composers including Yuzo Koshiro (he of the *Ys* scores) began to see their work recorded and sold to a rapidly increasing domestic fanbase and the occasional discerning importer from the West. Koshiro's recordings culminated in a 1991 release of a symphonic suite from his soundtrack to *ActRaiser*, a popular city-building simulator for the SNES. However big the domestic audience was, recordings of video game music were difficult to come by in territories outside Japan, and the appeal did seem limited for some years.

Nowadays, however, compilations and individual soundtrack scores on CD and digital formats regularly crash the classical charts with fervour and abandon. Thanks to the crossover success of Uematsu's *Final Fantasy* soundtracks (*Final Fantasy VIII* is perhaps his most notable recorded hit, having sold somewhere in the region of 400,000 copies worldwide since its release in 1999) and the demand for their recorded release in Western markets, there's now an entire industry dedicated to providing fans with high-quality recordings, easily the technical match of the finest film-score releases.

The rise of an industry

Instrumental in this process, in the UK at least, has been composer and arranger **Andrew Skeet** (born in 1969). A sometime member of the chamber-pop band The Divine Comedy and a provider of incidental music for TV hits such as *The Apprentice*, Skeet's career took a turn for the truly nerdy when he began work with the London Philharmonic Orchestra in 2011 (them again – they recorded Sugiyama's *Dragon Quest* score a full twenty-five years earlier). With Skeet on arranging and conducting duties, they came up with an album with the inventive title of *The Greatest Video Game Music*. It was a whistle-stop tour of the best-known video game music past and present, with superbly orchestrated versions of the 'hits' including Kondo's *Super Mario Bros.* theme and a suite from *The Legend of Zelda* alongside contemporary numbers such as *Metal Gear Solid*, *World of Warcraft* and, notably, composer Ari Pulkkinen's theme from the huge-selling smartphone-based game *Angry Birds* (remember that name – we'll come back to him later).

This combination of what had become 'standards' in the video game music genre and some modern and left-field choices was a sales winner – the album itself debuted at No. 23 in the Billboard 200. The last orchestral recording to get that high up the chart in its first week of release was Williams' *Star Wars Episode III: Revenge of the Sith,* so Skeet and the LPO were in exceedingly good company. This was proof that the market was indeed ready for video game music (though game soundtracks had been bothering the lower end of the charts for some years) and, importantly, that it was financially viable.

Skeet himself sounded a note of caution when the sequel to that compilation came out in 2012. Speaking to Classic FM in the run-up to its release, he admitted that video game music, though it had come a long way, wasn't held in the same regard as its more popular older cousin, film music: 'The music's maybe lagging behind the visuals in some games, but there's some lovely stuff. We're trying to show people what could be done.'

Still, the second release in the series, appropriately titled *The Greatest Video Game Music Vol. 2*, repeated the trick. Its mix of classics and modern innovators was another sales success story (and was available to purchase on a credit card-sized USB drive, if you so desired), providing further evidence that the tide had turned in favour of the gamers. An entire industry had sprung up and was proving to be a chart-winning formula at a time when recorded music sales were going through immense physical, digital and financial changes. Proof, as if it were needed, that the video game community was thoroughly dedicated to taking this music to a wider audience.

The Classic FM Hall of Fame:
Is VGM Really Classical?

Please forgive us as we blow our own trumpet a little, but the Classic FM Hall of Fame remains an excellent barometer for classical music in the UK. An annual survey of the nation's classical music listening preferences, it is essentially an enormous poll that ranks the public's favourite pieces of classical music, spanning the worlds of straight classical music from down the centuries (your Beethovens and your Bachs), film music (your John Barrys and your John Williamses) and, absolutely crucially to this book, video game music.

As you can imagine, it was not always this way. When the chart first started back in 1996, it was dominated by the leading lights of the classical establishment. Sitting pretty at No. 1 for the first five years of the chart was Max Bruch's effervescent *Violin Concerto*, and film music as a genre barely featured. As the years went on, movie music composers saw a shift in their favour as the genre became more popular, and big names such as John Williams, John Barry and Howard Shore started to crop up near the business end of the countdown. This shift continued and, now with over 100,000 votes each year, the chart looks set to continue to give us a pretty good picture of what the nation is listening to.

In 2012, video game music made itself known in the chart for the very first time. And not in a wimpy, propping-up-the-bottom-end kind of way, either. Straight in at No. 16 was perhaps the most popular video game music composer of all time, Nobuo Uematsu, with his soundtrack to *Final Fantasy VII*, sandwiched neatly between Pachelbel's *Canon* and Barber's *Adagio* for string orchestra. Millions of listeners heard the elegiac 'Aerith's Theme', probably for the first time, and reacted strongly. There were voices of support, of course, but there were nearly an equal number of the confused or the downright irate: the Internet was briefly ablaze, but the 'is video game music classical music?' debate was yet to have its day.

The following year saw a concerted social-media campaign put in place to try to get even more video game music further up the chart, headed by an enthusiast named Mark Robins. Robins, a PR man and game music oracle, engaged a legion of Facebook fans and Twitter followers in an attempt to boost the profile of video game music in the chart, focusing on a few key pieces.

In the end it worked and, for the first time in the history of the Hall of Fame, video game music went into the Top 5. Twice. Uematsu's *Final Fantasy* was there at No. 3, and Soule's music for *The Elder Scrolls* series was at No. 5. That wasn't all: **Grant Kirkhope**'s (born 1962) plaintive score for the gardening strategy game (yes, really) *Viva Piñata* also made a leap into the chart, landing at No. 174. These pieces not only announced (or bellowed, perhaps) the arrival of video game music in popular culture, but they also pushed Beethoven's *Piano Concerto No. 5* down into sixth place – and the establishment wasn't going to take it lying down.

Raging debates ensued in the natural battleground of the Internet age, the comments section of an online news story. Staunch classical fans, open-minded intermediates and vociferous gamers all joined in the robust debate, all discussing whether or not video game music deserved to be in the Hall of Fame at all, if *The Elder Scrolls* really was 'better' than Beethoven's *Piano Concerto No. 5*, or if the notion of an organised campaign to encourage voting was really in the right spirit. Composers James Hannigan, Jason Graves, Jack Wall and Garry Schyman (find out more about all of them later in the book) all got involved in the debate, using their distinct advantage of being alive over the likes of Beethoven to voice their satisfaction that video game music was getting a look-in.

The main thing, of course, was that no matter where the scores ended up in the chart, the debate was happening and video game music was crossing over into the mainstream. If you're so inclined, do have a read of the ensuing debate after the 2013 Hall of Fame – some of the comments for and against video game music's featuring in the chart have to be seen to be believed. You can find it in our video game music hub at ClassicFM.com/discover/video-game-music.

four

Video Game Music in the Concert Hall

If you go to a concert of video game music, you will see costumes. You will see gaggles of beautifully, elaborately and ornately dressed revellers, desperate to represent their favourite video game characters specifically for the moment when their theme will be played. And when the conductor whips the orchestra into that particular theme, there will be whooping, hollering and all brands of general concert frippery. There also may well be a giant video screen, displaying dazzling gameplay from whichever game's score is being played, with title screens alone prompting the audience to erupt into delirious cheers of recognition comparable to the reception to the Rolling Stones playing the first few licks of 'Start Me Up'. Basically, all the things that you would never see at a faithful, reverential recital of a Brahms symphony will be seen at a concert of video game music.

Besides the cultural (and, it has to be said, for the most part generational) shift, there are some other serious distinctions between the modern video game concert and the modern classical concert. For a start, video game concerts sell out. Fast. The first concert of Uematsu's *Final Fantasy* works, which was held at the Royal Albert Hall in London back in 2011, took three weeks to sell out. When the concert returned the following year, it took around two hours, which, frankly, is more like the ticket-buying reaction you'd expect to get if you suddenly announced a forthcoming show from Elvis Presley with a support slot from Freddie Mercury than a normal classical concert.

At present, concert venues across the UK are regularly playing host to video game concerts, from *re:PLAY: Symphony of Heroes* at London's Barbican Centre to the international touring phenomenon of

Video Games Live. What's more, they all feature some of the world's finest orchestras.

More and more, the live arena is considered one of the most important growth areas of the video game music industry. But how did this cultural phenomenon, this live juggernaut, emerge? Where were the seeds sown? Again, the answer lies in Japan.

Early Video Game Music Concerts

The first ever concert to feature music solely from video games took place in Tokyo, on 20 August 1987. The city's Suntory Hall was given over to the music of Sugiyama's first two *Dragon Quest* games, turned into symphonic suites, played by the Tokyo String Music Combination Playing Group and conducted by the composer himself. In what's more likely to be a quirk of translation than a genuine case of bad titling, the concert was named 'The Family Classic Concert'. Sugiyama masterminded the whole event and the subsequent concerts in the same series (eighteen of them in total), and they proved a hit every time.

For fans of the *Dragon Quest* games (of which there were evidently many), the thrill of hearing the scores from their favourite game played live by an orchestra, or at least a String Music Combination Playing Group, was huge. Just as home computers and consoles took video games out of the arcades and into the home, video game concerts were now taking the music from solitary bedrooms and living rooms across Japan back out to the communal world and, of all places, its concert halls.

As Popularity Grows, So Do the Programmes

As a result of this early success, concerts of video game music began to spread in popularity and frequency across Japan, with Sugiyama as something of a figurehead in organising them. His 'Family Classic' concerts soon spawned the 'Orchestral Game Concerts', which was a fully-fledged concert series made up of the game music of several different composers for the genre.

Beginning in 1991 and featuring the Tokyo City Philharmonic Orchestra, these new concerts featured a varied programme, representative of the then current state of Japanese video game music. So, Sugiyama's own *Dragon Quest III* and

IV kicked off the first of these concerts, but other popular pieces including Kondo's theme from *Super Mario Bros.* and *The Legend of Zelda: A Link to the Past* also featured, alongside Uematsu's *Final Fantasy IV*.

There were five of these concerts in total between 1991 and 1996, all of them with a different programme of music and a different orchestra. Composers were soon lining up to conduct their own works with top-notch orchestras, again proving that the secret to longevity in video game music was to take it out of the bedroom or the studio and into the concert hall.

In 1992, for instance, composer **Yoko Kanno** (born in 1964) took to the podium to conduct her music from Sega strategy game *Nobunaga's Ambition*, and 1995 saw an extended arrangement of Uematsu's music from *Final Fantasy VI*. Basically, the concerts were an accurate representation of the state of video game music in Japan in the early 1990s and, more importantly, an indicator that ticket sales could be healthy enough to carry the event over to Europe and America.

If you're looking for a flavour of what these now legendary concerts sounded like, then many of them are scattered across YouTube, ready for you to explore. However, if you're looking for an official recording of the shows, you might have to prepare yourself for a long and expensive journey. Recordings of all five concerts were made and commercially released, but their rarity is now legendary in video game music circles, spoken of with the same reverence that a Beatles fan might reserve for an undiscovered acetate recording of the Quarrymen.

Truly an enthusiast's genre, live shows of video game music continued to feed the fervour of its fanbase as it grew out of its Japanese origins.

The First European Concerts

Thomas Böcker (born in 1977), an adviser and producer of video game soundtracks in Germany, was watching the success of Sugiyama's Orchestral Game Concerts with great interest. Clearly inspired, he used his extensive contacts in the industry to mastermind a European version of the concerts, beginning in 2003 and tying in with the launch of the first ever European trade fair for video games, which was imaginatively titled 'GC – Games Convention'.

The venue was an absolute bastion of classical music performance, the Leipzig Gewandhaus concert hall, marking the long-awaited inception of video game music into the established halls of European classical music, and the Czech National Symphony Orchestra was the lucky ensemble tasked with bringing the scores to life.

Böcker's dream was that such events would engender the same reverence in Europe that video game fans in Japan were so clearly bringing to the concert hall. That first concert in 2003, titled 'Symphonic Game Music Concert', played it safe in terms of repertoire, and focused mostly on composers and works that had already featured in symphonic concerts before. The repertoire took in the likes of Uematsu's *Final Fantasy* (Uematsu himself was in attendance) and Soule's music for the video game version of *Harry Potter and the Chamber of Secrets*, mixed in with speeches and addresses from various members of the video game music community.

Some 2,000 people seemed to share Böcker's enthusiasm for live video game music and duly filled the Leipzig Gewandhaus on 20 August 2003, sixteen years to the day since Sugiyama's first ever 'Family

Classic Concert'. Böcker noted in his description of the event for gaming website Gamasutra that as much as it was a big step for the video game music world, it was also about getting its leading lights in a room together: 'A wonderful aspect of the event was that afterwards all the composers met at a restaurant to talk. Musicians from Germany, England, Sweden, the United States and Japan all sat down and shared their knowledge, experiences and passion for music.'

The concert became a firm fixture on the European concert scene and soon began to branch out: as well as a concert in Leipzig every year from 2003 to 2007, there were also events focusing on music from a number of specific franchises, including perhaps predictably an entire concert dedicated to the music of games from the now legendary Square stable (*Final Fantasy*, *Chrono Trigger* and the Disney–Square crossover hit *Kingdom Hearts*), again with cooperation and attendance from the composers themselves.

In 2009 the first Square concert, called Symphonic Fantasies, took place in Cologne's Philharmonic Hall; all the music was arranged into substantial suites, giving the whole show an air of the classical world. The show was broadcast on national radio, mastered at Abbey Road studios and unleashed on the record charts.

Further concerts began to hit London's Royal Albert Hall and Barbican venues with the Royal Philharmonic Concert Orchestra and London Symphony Orchestra heavily involved. The rest of Europe enjoyed a rich variety of events: Nintendo-only shows, *Final Fantasy* shows, Japanese-scores-only shows and dozens of other sell-out variations across the continent's greatest and most prestigious venues. The fans continued to shell out their hard-earned cash for a chance to see their gaming childhood – and their current gaming enthusiasms – brought to musical life, establishing a huge community of people experiencing orchestral music while dressed up as mythic warriors, folkloric, fantastical creatures and superhero-esque freedom fighters from their favourite games.

Increasingly, individual composers were jetted over from Japan to Europe to enjoy concerts featuring their own work. Big hitters such as Uematsu spend much of their time attending these concerts even now. Genre stalwarts such as **Yoko Shimomura** (born in 1967), best known for her scores for *Street Fighter II* and *Kingdom Hearts*, were overjoyed to discover that their music was being digested by a wider, international audience. Shimomura's own greatest-hits album, *Drammatica* (2008), received a full concert performance in 2009, performed by the Royal Stockholm Philharmonic Orchestra and conductor Arnie Roth (himself a key figure in the development of video game concerts). Live concerts were becoming chances for previously undiscovered heroes of the genre to get their moment in the spotlight, wherever in the world that spotlight might be.

Video Games Live

But what was the now thriving American video game music market doing all this time? Where was its series of sell-out orchestral shows in the country's swankiest venues, starring the country's best orchestras?

Well, composers **Tommy Tallarico** (born in 1968) and **Jack Wall** (born in 1964) were asking themselves the very same question in the early 2000s. Seeing the success of Thomas Böcker's Symphonic Game Music Concerts across Europe spurred the pair to create the distinctly better-titled 'Video Games Live' concerts, which kicked off in style at the Hollywood Bowl in 2005 with a none-too-shabby 11,000 punters in attendance to watch the Los Angeles Philharmonic.

Perhaps typically for the American incarnation of big-budget video game music shows, the Video Games Live shows feature incredibly impressive light shows and screen projections alongside occasional guitar solos from Tallarico himself (he's not known explicitly for his orchestral work, whereas Wall is a perhaps a more accomplished orchestrator and conductor).

In 2005, there were three separate Video Games Live shows. By 2009 that had ballooned into a globe-trotting tour of over seventy shows. Nowadays, the shows are booked up over a year in advance and the popularity doesn't seem to be on the wane.

Despite this distinctly more showbizzy take on the video games concert, what's pleasing about Tallarico's and Wall's venture is that they've kept classic game scores at the very heart of the fun. They take the audience all the way from orchestrated arcade classics such as *Frogger* and

Space Invaders up to the most recent releases, all beautifully arranged for symphony orchestra and choir.

Crucially, this is now a truly global event – concerts have made it back to Japan, gone through China, South Korea, Russia, South America, Europe and many of the states in America. Each new location proves the longevity of the genre and the interest of its fans.

The Future of Live Concerts

Live concerts of video game music might not have the omnipresence of classical concerts yet. But these huge events are only continuing to grow and attract new audiences to orchestral concerts.

Tellingly, more and more established orchestras are readily giving over their rehearsal and concert time to video game music concerts – due in no small part to the impressive ticket sales in an age of inconsistent attendance. Far from being a millstone around the orchestras' necks, feedback tends to show that the orchestras themselves love to stage concerts at which most of the attendees are not wearing ties. Unless that's part of their costume, of course.

The venues are continuing to get bigger and the budgets of the shows themselves are going up as well, which suggests that, for the time being, concerts of video game music could be an absolutely vital lifeline to ensure the future of live orchestral music.

five

Mobile Gaming, Online and the Future

Talking about the future of a genre that constantly works right at the bleeding edge of available consumer technology is always going to be, at best, a tad sketchy. Anyone reading this book even ten or twenty years from its publication will likely chuckle at its near-sightedness but, frankly, it's a risk we have to take when considering what the future has in store for video game music over the coming years.

What we can do in the meantime, before the embarrassment of technological advances takes hold, is take a look at the industry as it stands, with its multifarious and constant innovations and its rapidly increasing profile. It's safe to say that video game music has well and truly arrived across the world (not just in Japan), thanks to celebrity endorsements, fans that are willing to dress up as their favourite characters, mobile technology and an evolution in composition that means, more and more, the player is the one who controls the music – not just the composer.

Mobile Gaming

One of the greatest innovations in modern technology is undoubtedly the smartphone. But casting aside its general life-changing status for a moment, it's possible to see a huge effect on video games – the arrival of smartphones means that everyone now has a games console in their pockets and, therefore, potentially a bank of video game music to enjoy as well.

It's meant huge benefits for the composers themselves, too. Thanks to the advent of mobile gaming and specifically the arrival of the App Store from the tech behemoths at Apple, the job market has become an awful lot more accommodating for budding video game composers. Indeed, a study undertaken by SoundCon in 2013 showed that since the App Store opened for business in 2008 and iPhone owners were able to buy applications, the number of jobs for composers increased massively, so much so that game music became the third-fastest growing sector according to the US Bureau of Labor Statistics.

Perhaps the most notable beneficiary of this sudden upsurge in gainful employment was a Finnish composer named **Ari Pulkkinen** (born in 1982). Unlike his more famous musical countryman Jean Sibelius, Pulkkinen was not in the habit of composing epic symphonic poems destined for attention and legendary status down the centuries – instead, in the mid-noughties, he was eking out a living composing music for various video games, such as the desktop action game *Shadowgrounds* and the PlayStation 3 title *Super Stardust HD*. But then, in 2009, something happened – *Angry Birds* exploded onto the scene.

If you're not aware of *Angry Birds*, it's a mobile-based puzzle game in which the player controls the titular livid avian characters and attempts to stop a rampant herd of pigs trying to steal their eggs by hurling themselves at them from a catapult. Honestly. The main point here is that the game itself became a cultural phenomenon, with merchandise gracing toy shops on every continent and scores of bored commuters staring even harder into their laps as they tried to fend off those pesky pigs. And Pulkkinen's ridiculously catchy soundtrack became completely synonymous with the game's success.

The main theme from *Angry Birds* is a jaunty, folk-inspired loop of music, but it is ingeniously addictive (like the game) and perhaps indebted to the likes of *Tetris* in its knack for capturing the character of the game that spawned it. It's not orchestral in its original format, but thanks to the enthusiasts behind *The Greatest Video Game Music* album, Andrew Skeet and the London Philharmonic Orchestra, it became a fully orchestrated symphonic work in 2011 and the perfect advert for video game music in the twenty-first century.

Pulkkinen himself was so moved by the arrangement of his music for a full orchestra that he commented at the time: 'This is the first orchestral version of one of my compositions and it really comes alive. It has such a great depth and a majestic touch, and it was very emotional for me when I heard it the first time. I love it!'

Composing and Playing Apps

This continual democratisation of the technological world meant that any person could now own a high-powered games console in the shape of his or her smartphone. Even more impressive, though, it also meant people could use a smartphone to compose music of their own. Composing apps, which are designed to let users come up with their very own compositions, now range in sophistication from simple themes and instrument simulators to full-on, score-producing programmes that allow you to follow along with your magnum opus on screen.

Apps such as *Symphony Pro* are more like an industry tool that a conductor or a composer might use to jot down ideas on the way to and from rehearsal, or perhaps even orchestrate an entire symphony. At the other end of the spectrum, Apple's game-changing *GarageBand* allows you to turn your iPhone into a full, multi-track recording studio without even needing to be able to play an instrument at all.

Turning your smartphone or tablet into a piano, guitar, synthesizer or basically any kind of instrument at all is now a laughably simple technological feat and, in much the same way that the App Store turned everyone into console owners and games consumers, it makes composers out of all of us. It's this kind of advance in the field of video games (and so many of these composing apps really are like games) that has revolutionised the role of the composer – whether it's for symphony orchestra or folk trio, composers are no longer reliant on having years of conservatory schooling or, like Giacchino, taking evening classes in orchestration to get them up to speed with their contemporaries.

Online Gaming

As games moved inevitably towards the Internet, the scale of them completely changed. Just like the technical evolution that allowed gaming into the home and onto CDs and cartridges, the world of online gaming has opened up video game music to an even larger audience.

In particular, the arrival of Massively Multiplayer Online Games (MMOGs) has meant that, as long as you have an Internet connection, you can play video games against anyone in the world. There are stereotypes out there that envisage the players of these games to be archetypal, bedroom-dwelling nerds wearing headsets and bellowing obscenities at their fellow players across cyber-space, but the truth is, pleasingly, rather more elegant.

An extension of the MMOG genre is the Massively Multiplayer Online Role-Playing Game (MMORPG – these acronyms are coming thick and fast), essentially a huge network of gamers existing in the same online worlds, taking roles as characters and, to an extent, living a second life on the Internet. These games can attract literally millions of players worldwide, all essentially playing the same game, but with their own narrative to carve out.

It's interesting to note that, as far as video game music goes, it's this genre of MMORPGs that has perhaps encouraged the most interesting and forward-thinking music. Think about it: a role-playing game, just like *Final Fantasy*, is going to need music, but the gameplay could potentially last a lifetime. How on earth do you start composing music for something like that?

British composer **James Hannigan** (born in 1971) has done it all in video game music, and is still pushing the boundaries of the genre. He's scored movie tie-ins for the *Harry Potter* and *Lord of the Rings* series, had five Video Game BAFTA nominations, been a staff composer for Electronic Arts and also co-founded the Game Music Connect conference (more on that shortly). Not only that, he's one of a select few composers who has really relished the challenge of creating scores that can evolve with the gameplay and, particularly, how music works in online gaming.

His soundtrack for the MMORPG *RuneScape 3* is, he told Classic FM in 2013, something that consciously steps away from the film music genre and its constraints: 'The underlying technology forces you to think of the music in a slightly different way. You have to think in terms of how you can exploit that technology to offer interactive music. Longer-form music doesn't seem to match games very well.'

The funny thing is, Hannigan's soundtrack for this online game *does* sound like film music. It was recorded by the Slovak National Symphony Orchestra in a booming auditorium; it's got epic French horn themes and thunderous percussion duelling with more reflective, lyrical interludes ... basically all the traditional elements you might expect from a fantasy film soundtrack. But that underlying technology Hannigan mentioned is exactly why the music in *RuneScape* 3 is so innovative – actions in the game dictate exactly which bits of music you'll hear, meaning that each player (and there are hundreds of thousands, remember) could potentially have a completely different musical experience from the next. The musical implications of this technology are massive.

Interactive Music

In the heady, technologically dazzling world of twenty-first-century video games, composers are no longer expected to merely write music that has a beginning, middle and end. Games just aren't that simple: unlike a film, a player can take complete control of the action and often behave in non-linear, unpredictable ways, and the music has to fit in with that. Otherwise, your hero's majestic horn theme could well end up playing as he or she dangles precariously from a ledge, or some comic incidental music could be the soundtrack to their being pelted with slings and arrows.

These days, it's more a case of composing layers,

stems and fragments of music that can be repeated, embellished and adjusted automatically to reflect whatever the current user-defined gaming state is. So it's not exactly the most romantic of musical inspirations, but it has been the cause of some truly remarkable compositions.

Composers throughout the 1990s pioneered their own solutions to the problem of composing this truly 'interactive' music, painstakingly isolating each and every musical motif and assigning it to a very particular state of gameplay, be it combat, the difference between day and night, a victory dance or gradually heightening tension. Inevitably, this was an exhausting task for composers, especially if they had an impatient game developer on the other end of the phone.

Thankfully for modern composers, there are tools on hand to aid this delicate and time-consuming process of theme organisation. Companies like Audiokinetic and their flagship piece of software, the confusingly named Wwise, make it much easier to take all those high-quality orchestral snippets and layer them on top of each other to suit any mood or action. Modern narrative games with multifaceted plots and concepts require the soundtrack to react nimbly to the action – and the vast majority of composers now work in this fashion.

Even with these ingenious bits of kit to smooth the composition process along, however, composers increasingly must not only excel at their chosen musical discipline, but also become makeshift IT technicians and computer programmers.

Video Game Music Goes Truly Mainstream

It was perhaps only a matter of time before a bona-fide rock star took an interest in the industry. There were precedents, namely Trent Reznor of industrial metal band Nine Inch Nails, who provided music for the 1996 first-person action game *Quake*. But then in 2014, none other than former Beatle and occasional dabbler in classical music **Paul McCartney** (born in 1942) got in on the act. Back in 2009 he began work on a soundtrack to an online game named *Destiny* in collaboration with *Halo* composers O'Donnell and Salvatori, but the sheer scale of the project and, no doubt, McCartney's less-than-sedate schedule meant that the public didn't really hear anything about this huge coup until 2012.

Destiny is similar in scale and concept to *RuneScape 3* and its contemporaries, in that it can potentially house millions of online players. It's set in a futuristic, burned-out, apocalyptic future, where each player must battle for survival by defeating opponents in real time. McCartney's collaboration with O'Donnell and Salvatori resulted in a huge, war-movie-esque soundtrack, recorded by a 120-piece orchestra at the legendary Abbey Road studios (something of a second home for McCartney). It's densely written, bombastic and has the occasional choral interlude for good measure, but the most impressive thing is the sheer scale and professionalism of the whole operation.

McCartney contributed themes to the score, which O'Donnell and Salvatori then embellished and wove into a whole, but that wasn't all the former Beatle did. He also delivered a theme song, which isn't unheard of for a video game (Japanese releases like *Metal Gear Solid* have featured theme songs for credit sequences for years now), but the sheer magnitude of a star such as McCartney writing a song for a video game represents a peak in the art form. How much more mainstream can you get than Paul McCartney?

Unfortunately, the excitement around the soundtrack for *Destiny* was somewhat marred by O'Donnell's sudden firing from Bungie, the company behind the game. Just months before the soundtrack was due to be released to a fervent fanbase, O'Donnell tweeted, 'I'm saddened to say that Bungie's board of directors have terminated me without cause on April 11, 2014.' Reporting on the incident, *Forbes* magazine described it as being 'like Steven Spielberg firing John Williams. It just wouldn't happen.' Not much light has been cast on the ins and outs of this episode, but it does serve as a reminder that the video game music industry, though new and exciting and evolving at all times, is subject to the same industrial pressures as any other.

Trouble in Gaming Paradise?

Just as it seemed that video game music had truly arrived, fully-formed and accepted by the mainstream, something had to come along and ruin it. With a legion of new composers operating specifically in the video game music genre, there were inevitably problems – no games companies really knew how to pay their composers properly, apart from those hallowed and lucky enough to be staff composers, and the rapidly expanding recording industry for video game music was a whole other minefield to navigate.

American **Austin Wintory**, best known for his work on the innovative soundtrack for *Journey* (another online game, for the PlayStation Network), made public a rather thorny issue regarding his own employment union and their less-than-agreeable response to him writing a score for an independent game developer. In 2012, Wintory's union, the American Federation of Musicians, imposed new terms for composers working in the video game music medium. Simply put, those terms were put together without consulting AFM members and were roundly ignored or rejected by video game publishers – the result being a confusing limbo where composers were effectively unable to work on new scores.

Wintory, a keen advocate of independently produced games and a prolific composer despite the AFM's strict policies, was perhaps unlucky to be the one that the unions made an example of. They threatened him with a fine of $50,000 for his work on *The Banner Saga*, a game that was created by an independent developer and funded via Kickstarter, an online fundraising site that allows people to donate directly towards prospective creative projects at the very beginning of their development.

The composer was so incensed by what he saw as intimidation that he took to YouTube to voice his discontent. In a video that was viewed over 100,000 times within the first few months of posting it, Wintory railed against his union: 'This is about composers and musicians being able to work in a medium that we love without fear of threats and intimidation. It's about the next wave of musicians and composers … who shouldn't have to fear being attacked.'

At the time of writing this book, it's hard to say what the outcome will be as the dispute is still ongoing. However, what does seem evident is that a change is necessary to accommodate the humble video game music composer into a rapidly changing cultural landscape. The fact that, as an art form, video game music of this scale and nature is only a

few decades old means that many industry standards of the more established film music world are
simply not applied.

In a similar message of defiance, video game
music composers **Jesper Kyd** (born in 1972), James
Hannigan and **Jason Graves** (born in 1973) all
voiced their concerns about the amount of money
that professionals in their position actually get paid
compared with film composers, when speaking
at a conference named Game Music Connect in
2013 (we'll come to that below). Kyd in particular
emphasised the surprising differences in contrac-
tual benefits between the game and movie worlds:
'Film composers have more of a steady income …
Film composers do a bunch of films, and they get a
royalty cheque for their work every month. We don't
get that as game composers.'

Although it's unpleasant to wring these details
out of an industry that is so vibrant and focused on
the future, it does highlight exactly how far video
game music has to go. It's not quite the equal of film
music or contemporary classical music quite yet,
but with more and more composers (and ex-Beatles)
willing to make the leap over into the gaming world,
it's surely only a matter of time before some sort of

order is established and the composers can flourish creatively and financially, just like the industry that houses them.

The Future

Game Music Connect is the first video game music conference to be held in the UK. Its first incarnation in 2013 was held at the Purcell Room in the Southbank Centre, one of the bastions of the classical music establishment. Similar conferences have been held in recent years in the US, and other international video game conferences have also included an element of the music, but the arrival of GMC suggests an industrial shift is most definitely afoot. And who is at the epicentre of this particular movement?

Our old friend James Hannigan, along with fellow composer and game audio director **John Broomhall**, had a vision of aspiring games composers all coming together under one roof to learn more about the video game industry and how music fits into it, which came to pass at Game Music Connect. Composers including Graves and O'Donnell were on hand to tell attendees exactly what it was like to be a video game composer at the top of the industry, and to explain the challenges any prospective composers might face.

On paper, anything describing itself as a conference inevitably sounds a little dry, but it's an important development in the life of the genre – the fact that these events are now happening is indicative of a massive change in the scale of the industry.

Considering what's going to happen next in the world of video game music, the genre appears to have a bright future. It's currently cresting a wave of public interest and, looking at ticket sales in particular, shows little sign of crashing back into the ocean any time soon. What's more, the potential for video game music to progress is arguably far greater than many other genres of classical music at the moment. Film music, though it has its innovators still, is bound to the moving image and the cinema screen. Contemporary classical music continues, for the most part, to operate in the same way it has for the previous four or five centuries. Video game music, on the other hand, is still learning to walk – new games create new stimuli for composers, each technological advancement a new toy for them to play with and turn into an ingenious soundtrack

idea. As the genre now spirals off into myriad direc-
tions, it will be fascinating to see what the next
innovations will be.

The journey from the arcade, to the home, to
the concert hall is surely only the beginning.

six

20 Essential Video Game Music Scores

Looking for somewhere to start with video game music? This list of twenty scores encompasses the complete range, from colossal action scenes to reflective, emotional and even spooky themes from some of the most popular games in the industry's history. You can download highlights from this list at ClassicFM.com/handyguides.

Greg Edmonson: *Uncharted 2*

Edmonson's work on the *Uncharted* series began back in 2007 and followed his soundtrack to the cult sci-fi TV show *Firefly*. Indeed, the soundtrack to *Uncharted 2* won him a Video Game BAFTA, and it's fairly easy to see why. Combining traditional symphonic sounds with the distinctly Eastern sound of the *erhu* (sometimes known as 'the Chinese violin') lends the music an otherworldly, mystical quality that Edmonson really milks for all it's worth. The plot of the game follows protagonist Nathan Drake as he adventures his way, Indiana Jones-style, across the globe, and that atmosphere of derring-do is never far from the music.

Michael Giacchino: *Medal of Honor*

There's a definite nobility to the main theme of *Medal of Honor*, a characteristic that aligns Giacchino's soundtrack with the likes of Williams' score for *Born on the Fourth of July*, or perhaps even, at its most anguished, Samuel Barber's eternal *Adagio* for string orchestra. But, this being the world of video games, bombast, conflict and fireworks have to come into it, and indeed they do – Giacchino leavens the more violent sections of the score with deftness and sensitivity, despite our hero Lieutenant Jimmy Patterson being in almost constant mortal danger. If you like your game music to sound like film music, this is the score for you.

Jason Graves: *Tomb Raider*

Perhaps even the most transient of video game observers will know *Tomb Raider*. Initially quite a silly but well-loved series of adventure games in the late 1990s, it received a far more mature and serious reboot in 2013, and composer Graves was the man to provide the soundtrack for lead character Lara Croft's triumphant return to the gaming world. When he spoke to Classic FM about the project, he described it as 'the most open-ended, creative, collaborative project I've ever worked on'. It shows – this has to be one of the most all-encompassing and experimental soundtracks for a mainstream game released so far.

Harry Gregson-Williams: *Metal Gear Solid 2: Sons of Liberty*

A fine pedigree in action-movie soundtracks prepped Harry Gregson-Williams for his work on *Metal Gear Solid 2: Sons of Liberty*, and you can really hear those influences seeping into the percussion-heavy cues that propel the gameplay. There's a certain degree of ambience, sections of electronic pulsing and buzzing, but when these combine with Gregson-Williams' superb orchestral writing, the effect is more than just two genres being welded together. In the context of the game (a high-tech espionage thriller), it's completely breathtaking stuff, not to be dismissed as just a bizarre fusion or simply a transfer of action-movie tactics to video games.

James Hannigan: *RuneScape 3*

Kicking off with devilishly trilling woodwinds, huge-sounding French horns and generally leaking orchestral expertise from every pore, *RuneScape 3* is Hannigan's magnum opus. His work on franchises such as the *Harry Potter* game series is evident as he stridently uses every trick in the book to make this open-world game really sound as big as it potentially could be. And, even more remarkably, the music for this game has to serve many functions – it's integral to each individual player's journey, but it also has to be listenable in its own right. Somehow, Hannigan cracks it. The gentle harp-and-violin duet that kicks off the 'Waterfall II' cue is particularly enchanting, if you're looking for somewhere to start.

Yoko Kanno: *Nobunaga's Ambition*

Another tricky one to track down, but if you're willing to trawl YouTube then you'll be rewarded with a lush, filmic series of themes punctuated by sharp snare rattles and Williams-esque flourishes. Kanno has spent a lot of her career composing for Japanese cinema, specifically anime, and it really shows. There's an almost endless series of instalments in this series of games (which is a turn-based strategy franchise), which makes narrowing it down to one excerpt a bit tricky, but the whole lot is worth a serious binge-listen.

Grant Kirkhope: *Viva Piñata*

It's a nonsensical-seeming game aimed at children, but *Viva Piñata*'s soundtrack has become something even more accessible. What North Yorkshire native Grant Kirkhope did with his main theme for the game (an open-ended strategy game in which players must cultivate a successful garden, populated by living Piñata creatures) was to make it as approachable, charming and downright affable as possible. If you're looking for touchstones, think of Giacchino's music for Disney–Pixar's *Up*, or a fresh-faced John Barry work. The plaintive, inviting melody of 'Oven-Fresh Day' in particular is worth repeat plays – we absolutely defy you not to be wistfully moved by the end.

Yuzo Koshiro: *Shenmue*

Shenmue was a game-changer when it was released on Sega's Dreamcast in 1999, featuring real recorded voice acting (rather than the on-screen text of *Final Fantasy*), cinematic graphics and – of course – a huge, sweeping orchestral score. There's something almost *Gone with the Wind*-esque about the swooshing gongs and elaborate orchestration that Koshiro uses, lending *Shenmue* a rare legendary status in the industry. It was a signal that things were moving forward in the genre as a whole, and the music was going to have to become every bit as cinematic, intricate and inventive as the visuals.

Koji Kondo: *The Legend of Zelda*

Indispensable to the video game music genre, Kondo's *The Legend of Zelda* soundtracks are, all of them, charmingly homespun, winsome and – believe it or not – definite cousins of Howard Shore's soundtracks to the *Lord of the Rings* movie trilogy. As the series progressed through its various instalments, Kondo's craft became progressively more sophisticated until the music itself actually became integral to the gameplay. Listen out for the way he uses flutes in particular to echo music that players have to learn and play themselves in order to progress.

Jesper Kyd: *Hitman 2: Silent Assassin*

Danish composer Jesper Kyd enlisted the help of 110 musicians and singers of the Budapest Symphony Orchestra and Choir to give the big-budget feel necessary for the second instalment of the popular *Hitman* franchise. A sort of James Bond clone with no hair, the Hitman himself uses stealth and occasional bursts of extreme violence to ensnare his targets, and Kyd does exactly the same thing with the music. The tension is, at times, unbearably yet beautifully constructed, and those violent moments are indeed reflected in the score. Exciting, atmospheric stuff.

Yasunori Mitsuda: *Chrono Trigger*

The *Chrono Trigger* series of games are nothing short of legendary in gaming circles, so it's only appropriate that the soundtracks are given the same respect. Yasunori Mitsuda's themes are comparable to those of Uematsu in the *Final Fantasy* series (in fact, Uematsu assisted Mitsuda in arranging certain sections of the *Chrono Trigger* score) and have gone on to be a frequent and popular inclusion to many live concerts of video game music. The soundtracks themselves have also seen numerous re-releases over the years as sequels have come and gone, making it a stalwart of the genre.

Martin O'Donnell and Michael Salvatori: *Halo*

If there was one particular theme that the video game community might describe as being absolutely emblematic of the genre, O'Donnell's and Salvatori's main theme for *Halo* might well be it. It oozes epic sophistication from the outset. With doom-laden choral writing, crawling towards serious bombast and Hollywood-blockbuster orchestral fireworks, that theme and the full soundtrack that unfurls after it were an early example of the impressive effect video game music can have on an audience.

Garry Schyman: *Bioshock*

American Garry Schyman is an interesting character in the video game world. After making his first video game soundtrack in 1993, he gave it a couple of years before declaring the medium unfit for purpose. Tellingly, when he returned to the genre many years later, he was hailed as a modern master, with scores such as *Bioshock* showing exactly why. The tense, explosive and action-packed soundtrack is the perfect accompaniment to the game's aesthetic and feel, which, much more than Schyman's early experiences in the game industry, really do display the capabilities of the genre.

Yoko Shimomura: *Kingdom Hearts*

If Shimomura's music weren't distinctive enough on its own, it'd be worth noting that she is one of the very few female composers to have made a huge mark on the video game music industry. Thanks to her beautiful, emotionally wrought music for the *Kingdom Hearts* series in particular, she's already been written into the history of the genre. If you're looking for a place to start with her, the first *Kingdom Hearts* original soundtrack is as good as any, chock-full of dainty piano lines and sympathetic, sensitively composed orchestral accompaniment, showing no little influence from the likes of Rachmaninov and Ravel.

Jeremy Soule: *The Elder Scrolls V: Skyrim*

There's so much to listen out for in *Skyrim*, not least of all the bizarre but inspired chorusing of a choir in an entirely made-up language used in the game itself, called 'Draconic'. That track, 'Dragonborn', uses a thirty-strong choir layered three times to create the effect of ninety voices singing, with booming orchestral support throughout. The soundtrack for *Skyrim* clocks in at a whopping 200 minutes in total, which perhaps gives an idea of the scale of the game itself and proves that video game composers often have to work a little harder and longer than their counterparts in the movie world.

Koichi Sugiyama: *Dragon Quest*

The elder statesman of video game music, Sugiyama was instrumental in taking the genre into an orchestral setting. Symphonic suites of his music have since been created for concert performance, and later entries in the franchise have utilised full orchestral forces, but the charm of this embryonic, beautifully melodic series of themes trumps them all. You might struggle to find a recording of the original soundtrack played by an orchestra, but a trawl of YouTube might prove fruitful.

Christopher Tin: *Civilisation IV*

The *Civilisation* games are, as the title suggests, all

about creating and maintaining a group of people on a huge scale. So how do you go about summing up the struggle of humanity towards survival, staving off extinction and building a prosperous future in music? Well, American composer **Christopher Tin** (born 1976) had a bash at it with 'Baba Yetu', a Karl Jenkins-esque retelling of the Lord's Prayer in Swahili. It's a superb example of just how diverse video game music can be, and proof that it needn't just be a crashing accompaniment to people getting blown up. Tin's world-music-inspired soundtrack has, unsurprisingly, become a genre classic, with 'Baba Yetu' even being performed at the United Nations General Assembly.

Nobuo Uematsu: *Final Fantasy VII*

He's a legend of video game music and the biggest hitter in the Classic FM Hall of Fame, but when he spoke to Classic FM in 2012, on the eve of another sell-out live performance of his music for various *Final Fantasy* scores at London's Royal Albert Hall, Uematsu was a little coy about his own success: 'At the time I created "Aerith's Theme", I thought it was a good piece …' His coyness is completely misplaced, though – as we established earlier in this book, the score for the whole of *Final Fantasy VII* is superbly cinematic. Not all of it lends itself to orchestral interpretation and the MIDI sounds of its original recording do date it, but the melodies have proved as timeless as those of any of Uematsu's Hollywood counterparts.

Jack Wall: *Mass Effect*

He's perhaps better known, along with Tommy Tallarico, as the man behind the now legendary Video Games Live concert tour, but Jack Wall's scores for the *Mass Effect* series have guaranteed his slot in the pantheon of video game music greats. The first instalment was, in fact, composed with Wall as figurehead of a team of composers (including Richard Jacques, who went on to score tie-ins for the James Bond franchise. Wall & Co.'s brutalist score takes its cues from the likes of Vangelis, providing an electronic edge to some pretty tasty orchestral writing.

Austin Wintory: *Journey*

Journey was something of a game-changer, if you'll excuse the pun. A critical hit and a beacon of independent gaming taking on the big guns of the industry, Wintory's score ingeniously reacts to the player's movements, meaning that musical themes are built up by each player as his or her game progresses. Players can interact with each other only by sounding a musical chime (taking Kondo's use of flute themes in the *Zelda* games to the next level), and gradually a cello theme comes to represent each individual. As Wintory himself described it (before snaffling a haul of awards for his work), it's 'a big cello concerto where you are the soloist and all the rest of the instruments represent the world around you'.

About Classic FM

If this series of books has whetted your appetite to find out more, one of the best ways to discover what you like about classical music is to listen to Classic FM. We broadcast a huge breadth of classical music 24 hours a day across the UK on 100–102 FM, on DAB digital radio, online at ClassicFM.com, on Sky Channel 0106, on Virgin Media channel 922 and on FreeSat channel 721. You can also download the free Classic FM app, which will enable you to listen to Classic FM on your iPhone, iPod, iPad, Blackberry or Android device.

As well as being able to listen online, you will find a host of interactive features about classical music, composers and musicians on our web-site, ClassicFM.com. When we first turned on

Classic FM's transmitters more than two decades ago, we changed the face of classical music radio in the UK for ever. Now, we are doing the same online.

The very best way to find out more about which pieces of classical music you like is by going out and hearing a live performance by one of our great British orchestras for yourself. There is simply no substitute for seeing the whites of the eyes of a talented soloist as he or she performs a masterpiece on stage only a few feet in front of you, alongside a range of hugely accomplished musicians playing together as one.

Classic FM has a series of partnerships with orchestras across the country: the Bournemouth Symphony Orchestra, the London Symphony Orchestra, the Orchestra of Opera North, the Philharmonia Orchestra, the Royal Liverpool Philharmonic Orchestra, the Royal Northern Sinfonia and the Royal Scottish National Orchestra. And don't forget the brilliant young musicians of the National Children's Orchestra of Great Britain and of the National Youth Orchestra of Great Britain. To see if any of these orchestras have a concert coming up near you, log onto our website at ClassicFM.com and click on the 'Concerts and

Events' section. It will also include many other classical concerts – both professional and amateur – that are taking place near where you live.

Happy listening!

About the Author

Daniel Ross is a Senior Content Editor for Classic FM Interactive, the online platform of Global Radio's national classical music station, Classic FM.

After gaining a music degree from Royal Holloway, University of London, in 2007, he began his writing career by contributing interviews, reviews and features to various pop and rock magazines and websites before joining Classic FM in 2012.

Working at Classic FM has given him first-hand access to some of the most important and influential figures in the world of video game music. He has also attended various video game music concerts and events as the genre has made its mark in the UK.

Index

Abbey Road studios,
    London 47, 64
Abrams, J. J. 21
ActRaiser 30
Ambition 76–77
Angry Birds 32, 55–56
App Store 54–55
Apple 54, 57–58
Artistry Entertainment
    26
Audiokinetic 62

Bach, Johann Sebastian
    34
Barber, Samuel 24;
    Adagio 35, 74
Barbican, London 47
Barry, John 34, 77

Beethoven, Ludwig van
    xi, 27, 34, 37; *Piano
    Concerto No. 5* 36
Bioshock 80–81
Böcker, Thomas 44–46,
    48
Bournemouth Symphony
    Orchestra 88
Brahms, Johannes 40
Broomhall, John 69
Bruch, Max, *Violin
    Concerto* 34
Budapest Symphony
    Orchestra and Choir
    79
Bungie 65

Capcom 23

CDs 4, 9–10, 18, 30–31, 58

Christopherson, Jamie 22

Chrono Trigger 46, 79–80

Civilisation IV 82–83

Commodore 64 3

concerts 40, 41–42, 44–48

consoles 3–4, 9, 54

Czech National Symphony Orchestra 45

Destiny 63–65

Dig Dug 3

Disney 19, 21, 46, 77

Donkey Kong 6

Dragon Quest 30, 32, 41, 82; *I* 4; *III* 42; *IV* 43

Dreamcast 14, 77

Edmondson, Greg 73–74

Elder Scrolls, The x–xi, 36; *III* 26; *V: Skyrim* 26, 81–82

Famicom 3, 5

Family Classics 42, 45–46

Final Fantasy x, 4, 8–9, 14, 25, 27, 31, 36, 40, 41, 45–47, 59, 77, 79; *VI* 43; *VII* 10–13, 35, 83–84; *VIII* 31

FMVs (Full Motion Videos) 12–13

Frogger 2, 49

Game Music Connect 60, 68–69

GarageBand 57

GC (Games Convention) 44

Giacchino, Michael 19–21, 27, 58, 74, 77; *Alias* 21; *Lost* 19, 21; *Planet of the Apes* 19; *Star Trek* 19, 21; *The Incredibles* 19; *The Lion King* 19; *Up* 19, 21, 77

God of War 41

Gone with the Wind 77

Graves, Jason 36, 68, 69, 75

Gregson-Williams, Harry 22, 75–76

Halo 24–25, 41, 63, 80

Hannigan, James 36, 59–60, 68, 69, 76

Harry Potter 27, 45, 60, 76

Hendrix, Jimi 12

Herrmann, Bernard 24

Hibino, Norihiko 22

Hitchcock, Alfred: *North by Northwest* 24; *Psycho* 24

Hitman 2: Silent Assassin 79

Hollywood Bowl 49

interactive music 61–63

Jacques, Richard 84

Jenkins, Karl 83

John, Elton 8

Jonami 2

Journey 66, 84–85

Kai, Toshio 1

Kaida, Akari 23

Kanno, Yoko 43, 76–77

Kickstarter 67

Kingdom Hearts 46, 48, 81

Kirkhope, Grant 36, 77

Kondo, Koji 4, 5–8, 17, 32, 43, 85, 78–79

Koshiro, Yuzo 14, 15, 17, 30, 78

Kyd, Jesper 68, 79

Legend of Zelda, The x, 5–8, 32, 85, 78–79; *A Link to the Past* 43

Leipzig Gewandhaus 45

London Philharmonic Orchestra 4, 31, 32, 56

London Symphony Orchestra 88

Lord of the Rings 60

Los Angeles Philharmonic 49

Lost World: Jurassic Park, The 20, 21, 26

Mass Effect 84

Massively Multiplayer Online Games (MMOG) 58–59

Massively Multiplayer Online Role-Playing Games (MMORPG) 59, 60

McCartney, Paul 63–65

Medal of Honor 21, 74
Metal Gear Solid 22–23, 32, 64; *2: Sons of Liberty* 75–76
MIDI 11, 84
Mitsuda, Yasunori 79–80
mobile gaming 54–56

Moroder, Giorgio 24

N64 11
Namco 3
National Children's Orchestra of Great Britain 88
National Youth Orchestra of Great Britain 88
New Japan Philharmonic Orchestra 24
NHK Symphony Orchestra 30
Nintendo 3, 5–6, 11, 47; Entertainment System (NES) 4, 5; Super Nintendo Entertainment System (SNES) 4, 9, 30
Nishigaki, Syun 24
Nishikado, Tomohiro 2
Nobunaga's Ambition 43

Northerner: Soule Symphony No. 1 27

O'Donnell, Martin 24, 63–65, 69, 80
online gaming 58–61
Orchestra of Opera North 88
Orchestral Game Concerts 44
orchestras 22–25

Pachelbel, Johann, *Canon* 35
Pac-Man 1
Philharmonia Orchestra 88
Philharmonic Hall, Cologne 46
Pixar 21, 77
PLAY: Symphony of Heroes 40
PlayStation 10, 11, 20, 24, 55, 66
Pokémon 6
Pulkkinen, Ari 32, 55–56
Purcell Room, London 69

Quake 63

Rachmaninov, Sergei 81
Ravel, Maurice 81;
    Boléro 7
Resident Evil 23–24;
    II 23; *III: Nemesis* 24
Reznor, Trent 63
Robins, Mark 35
Romero, George 23
Roth, Arnie 48
Royal Albert Hall, London
    40, 47, 83
Royal Liverpool
    Philharmonic
    Orchestra 88
Royal Northern Sinfonia
    88
Royal Philharmonic
    Concert Orchestra
    40, 47
Royal Scottish National
    Orchestra 88
Royal Stockholm
    Philharmonic
    Orchestra 48
RPGs 4, 6, 9
RuneScape 3 60–61, 64,
    76

Salvatori, Michael 24,
    63–64, 80

Saturn 11, 20
Schyman, Garry 36,
    80–81
scores 17–27
Secret of Evermore 25
Sega 11, 14, 20, 43, 77;
    Mega Drive 9
Shadowgrounds 55
Shenmue 14, 77
Shimomura, Yoko 47–48,
    81
Shore, Howard 34; *Lord
    of the Rings* 78
Sibelius, Jean 55
Skeet, Andrew 31, 33, 56
Slovak National
    Symphony Orchestra
    60
Sonic the Hedgehog ix
Sony 10, 11, 20, 23;
    see also PlayStation
Soule, Jeremy x, 25–27,
    45, 81–82; *see also
    Northerner: Soule
    Symphony No. 1*
Space Invaders 2, 50
Spielberg, Steven 20, 65
Square 8, 25, 46
Star Wars 27
Stravinsky, Igor 12

Street Fighter II 48

String Music
  Combination Playing
  Group 41–42

Sugiyama, Koichi 4, 8,
  10, 17, 30, 32, 41, 42,
  44, 45, 82

Suntory Hall, Tokyo 41

Super Mario Bros. ix,
  4–6, 32, 43

Super Stardust HD 55

Symphonic Fantasies 46

Symphonic Game Music
  Concerts 45, 48

Symphony Pro 57

Taito 2

Tallarico, Tommy 48–49

Tetris 56

Tin, Christopher 82–83

Tokyo Philharmonic
  Orchestra 30, 42

Tomb Raider 75

Tomozawa, Makoto 23

Total Annihilation 26

Uchiyama, Shusaku 24

Ueda, Masami 23, 24

Uematsu, Nobuo x, 4,
  8–13, 15, 17, 27, 31,
  35, 36, 40, 45, 47, 79,
  83–84

Uncharted 2 73–74

Vangelis 84

Video Games Live 49, 84

Viva Piñata 36, 77

Wagner, Richard 8–9, 12

Wall, Jack 36, 48–49, 84

Wembley Stadium,
  London 40

Williams, John 12, 18–19,
  27, 34, 65, 77; *Born on
  the Fourth of July* 74;
  ET: The Extra-Terrestrial
  17, 18; *Harry Potter*
  18; *Indiana Jones* 18;
  Jurassic Park 10;
  Superman 5, 18; *Star
  Wars* 17, 18

Wintory, Austin 66–67,
  84–85

World of Warcraft 32

Wwise 62

Ys 30; *I: Ancient Ys
  Vanished* 14

Zimmer, Hans 22

In the same series

The Classic FM Handy Guide to Classical Music
by Darren Henley

The Classic FM Handy Guide to The Orchestra
by Darren Henley

The Classic FM Handy Guide to Classical Recordings by Sam Jackson

The Classic FM Handy Guide to Ballet
by Tim Lihoreau

The Classic FM Handy Guide to Film Music
by Rob Weinberg

The Classic FM Handy Guide to Opera
by Rob Weinberg